KEEPING THE CUTTING EDGE:

Setting and Sharpening Hand and Power Saws

by Harold "Dynamite" Payson

Photographs by Jeff Julian
Illustrations by Sam Manning

WoodenBoat
BOOKS
Brooklin, Maine USA

Published by WoodenBoat Books
Naskeag Road, PO Box 78
Brooklin, Maine 04616 USA
www.woodenboatbooks.com

ISBN 13: 978-0-937822-02-9
ISBN 10: 0-937822-02-7

Cover photograph by Kip Brundage

Library of Congress Cataloging in Publication Data

Payson, Harold H.
        Keeping the cutting edge.
        1. Saw-filing.   2. Saws—Maintenacne and
repair.   I. Title.
T1235.P3   1985   621.9′3   85-6504
ISBN 0-937822-02-7 (pbk.)

Printed in Canada by Friesens

15 14 13 12 11 10

S aw filing is certainly an art, but it's no mystery. Saws still cut the same today as they did when they were invented back in the dim past. Take a little time with me, and I will pass on the few basics of what you can do to make your saw cut properly — how to start and when to start, the skills you'll need to make your saw *saw*, and what to look for when it does not.

I was about 20 years old before I decided to learn to file my own saws. I had got into the habit of lugging them to my father, who did them uncomplainingly along with the ones he got paid for doing as a professional filer. It occurred to me that I was going to feel pretty guilty when I got to 50 if I was still dumping dull saws on my 80-year-old father.

It takes time to develop the coordination of hand and eye needed for saw sharpening work, so don't be disappointed if you don't learn overnight. It took me a year of filing, off and on, before my father and teacher, H.W. Payson, finally squinted along the edge of my handsaw masterpiece and said: "That is as good as I can do" — words I never thought I'd hear. My nephew Ashley Post, on the other hand, did a fine job the first time around.

HANDSAWS

Let's establish some of the fundamentals before we begin. Whether hand or power, straight, band, or circular, saws are designed for just two kinds of cutting—across the grain, and with the grain. Crosscut teeth act like tiny chisels, taking out slices across the grain that chamber in the tooth gullets and are spewed out on the push stroke of the handsaw. Uniformity of height of teeth, the amount of bevel on the face of the teeth, and how much they rake ahead or back, plus the amount of set, all play a part in the ability of the saw to cut.

Ripsaws cut with the grain, and the teeth, instead of having a chisel or slicing action, work more like hammers. They simply knock out the wood fibers, which is why their teeth are filed flat across their tops and faces and present a square edge for just that job.

Here's one tip that perhaps you can use right away to save yourself future trouble, even before you've read this whole manual. Don't take a single stroke with that new saw you just bought, or the one you're buying tomorrow, without following this suggestion:

Lay your virgin-pure saw on a good stiff piece of paper and make a fine-line tracing around its teeth. Then hang the tracing in your shop, or stow it safely, against the day when you first try your hand at sharpening that saw.

The reason? Because whether it's a small handsaw, a circular saw, or a large cordwood saw, its teeth are correctly shaped when it leaves the factory. If you know nothing at all about tooth shape, your tracing will show you exactly the remedy required when you try to bring it back to its original configuration.

Correct sharpening of any saw involves three operations: jointing, setting, and filing. That order is never varied unless the professional filer decides, based on his own experience, that a given saw needs only one, or perhaps two, of those operations.

JOINTING AND SETTING

Jointing is easily understood; it's obvious that all the teeth must be of equal height for all of them to cut. Setting offsets alternate teeth to one side or the other, bending one tooth slightly to the right and the next slightly to the left. This ensures that the teeth will cut a kerf that is slightly wider than the flat part of the blade; this eliminates pinching if you saw straight and true.

I suggest that right now you dig out a needle, and with it check any handsaw you possess to see if it has the proper set. Hold the saw, teeth up, with the small end in a vise or resting on some stable surface, and the handle, at your end, slightly elevated. Lay the needle in the vee between the alternately offset teeth, near the handle. It should slide as though it were riding in a trough, all the way down to the lower end. And *that* is the proper set.

Take the saw I talk about in "Rejuvenating an Old Saw" (page 12). Mr. Fickett passed it to me after he had given my blank a set of teeth. When I cast my eye along the row of those newly cut teeth, it was obvious that his machine had done a good job of producing teeth of uniform size and height, and it looked as though I could get away with omitting the jointing process and needed only to set the teeth and file them.

But just to make sure, I picked up my jointer, a hand-held device about 5" long and 2" deep that holds a file. A light sweep over the whole length of the toothed edge showed that they were indeed uniform, for it took about

Carpenters' handsaws—basic tooth patterns—

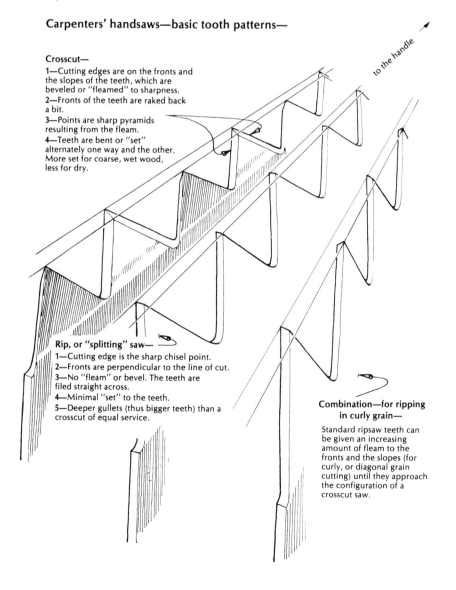

to the handle

Crosscut—
1—Cutting edges are on the fronts and the slopes of the teeth, which are beveled or "fleamed" to sharpness.
2—Fronts of the teeth are raked back a bit.
3—Points are sharp pyramids resulting from the fleam.
4—Teeth are bent or "set" alternately one way and the other. More set for coarse, wet wood, less for dry.

Rip, or "splitting" saw—
1—Cutting edge is the sharp chisel point.
2—Fronts are perpendicular to the line of cut.
3—No "fleam" or bevel. The teeth are filed straight across.
4—Minimal "set" to the teeth.
5—Deeper gullets (thus bigger teeth) than a crosscut of equal service.

Combination—for ripping in curly grain—
Standard ripsaw teeth can be given an increasing amount of fleam to the fronts and the slopes (for curly, or diagonal grain cutting) until they approach the configuration of a crosscut saw.

the same amount off the tops of all the teeth. Once across was all that was needed for that job, as compared to the many passes that are required with saws whose teeth are badly out of shape. When the teeth are very uneven after an unskilled filer has produced some big and some little teeth, after a few passes with the jointer you will see that some have large flat spots where much metal has been taken off, while the short ones have hardly been touched at all. Though the whole idea of jointing is to mow all the teeth down to the same height, common sense must be applied. If there are a few teeth that have been filed to near oblivion, it doesn't make sense to take all the rest down to their size.

Remember that the more you joint the teeth down, the more work you make for yourself. To see how much

that can amount to, just keep looking at the teeth that were the highest and see how much wider their tops have become, and how much filing you will have to do on those flattened tops before they will ever cut again. You can imagine what my first saw-filing attempts looked like—big teeth, little teeth, joint them all down, and file them again.

The jointing process is done first not only to provide a uniform height for filing but to provide it for setting as well. I've touched on tooth set earlier. Sawing without set in the teeth is like trying to cut a squash with a butcher knife. Every time I've done that, the knife goes in and binds, I pound and bang at it, then I curse, and finally I take the thing out to the shop and have at it with a hatchet.

Similarly, because the cutting edge

of a saw without set is no wider than the blade, it bogs down when the blade starts to bury in the wood; then the wood pinches it. Push harder, push until blue of face if you will, and you'll put a kink in your saw, and maybe one in your gut, too.

So you'll need to have a saw set—a small hand-held tool that pushes a plunger against the saw tooth to bend it over a small anvil, all of which action takes place inside the tool. The anvil sits in a slot, and you can adjust it up and down by means of a screw knob in order to select the amount of the set. This depends on how high or low the tooth hits the bevel of the anvil.

Saw sets come in two styles: pistol grip and straight. I find the pistol grip much more comfortable to use; it also allows me to see what I am doing.

Shape of teeth in a hand crosscut saw—

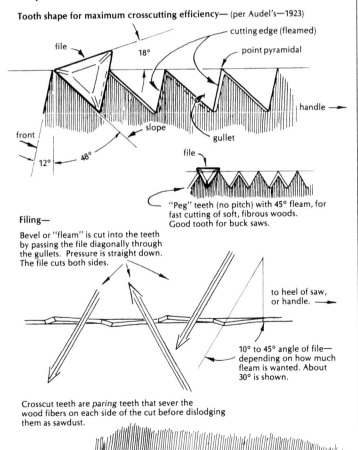

Tooth shape for maximum crosscutting efficiency— (per Audel's—1923)

file · 18° · cutting edge (fleamed) · point pyramidal · handle · slope · gullet · front · 12° · 48° · file

"Peg" teeth (no pitch) with 45° fleam, for fast cutting of soft, fibrous woods. Good tooth for buck saws.

Filing—

Bevel or "fleam" is cut into the teeth by passing the file diagonally through the gullets. Pressure is straight down. The file cuts both sides.

to heel of saw, or handle. →

10° to 45° angle of file—depending on how much fleam is wanted. About 30° is shown.

Crosscut teeth are *paring* teeth that sever the wood fibers on each side of the cut before dislodging them as sawdust.

Teeth-points describe parallel track at the beginning of the cut.

Hand ripsaws—

Shape of teeth—

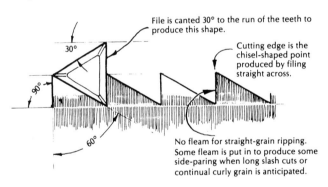

File is canted 30° to the run of the teeth to produce this shape.

30° · 90° · 60°

Cutting edge is the chisel-shaped point produced by filing straight across.

No fleam for straight-grain ripping. Some fleam is put in to produce some side-paring when long slash cuts or continual curly grain is anticipated.

Filing—

Straight across, from alternate sides, in order to ensure that any bevel accidentally applied does not occur on one side of the saw only.

Pressure on the file is more or less aimed at the root of the gullet, favoring the side that helps regulate, or equalize, the size and shape of the teeth.

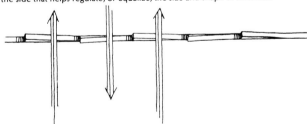

Ripsaw teeth make a gouging cut. Their "sawdust" is small block shavings.

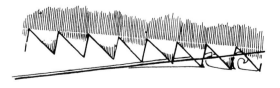

"Jointing" a handsaw—

(to cut the points of all teeth down to one height)

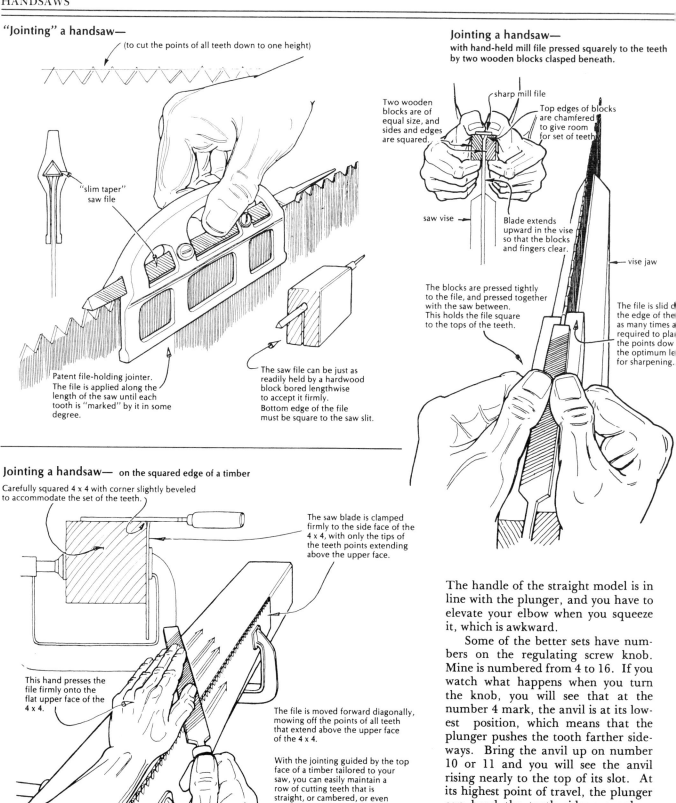

"slim taper" saw file

Patent file-holding jointer. The file is applied along the length of the saw until each tooth is "marked" by it in some degree.

The saw file can be just as readily held by a hardwood block bored lengthwise to accept it firmly. Bottom edge of the file must be square to the saw slit.

Jointing a handsaw—

with hand-held mill file pressed squarely to the teeth by two wooden blocks clasped beneath.

sharp mill file

Two wooden blocks are of equal size, and sides and edges are squared.

Top edges of blocks are chamfered to give room for set of teeth

saw vise

Blade extends upward in the vise so that the blocks and fingers clear.

vise jaw

The blocks are pressed tightly to the file, and pressed together with the saw between. This holds the file square to the tops of the teeth.

The file is slid d the edge of the as many times a required to pla the points dow the optimum le for sharpening.

Jointing a handsaw— on the squared edge of a timber

Carefully squared 4 x 4 with corner slightly beveled to accommodate the set of the teeth.

The saw blade is clamped firmly to the side face of the 4 x 4, with only the tips of the teeth points extending above the upper face.

This hand presses the file firmly onto the flat upper face of the 4 x 4.

The file is moved forward diagonally, mowing off the points of all teeth that extend above the upper face of the 4 x 4.

With the jointing guided by the top face of a timber tailored to your saw, you can easily maintain a row of cutting teeth that is straight, or cambered, or even curved to a radius—as is required for a two-man felling saw.

The handle of the straight model is in line with the plunger, and you have to elevate your elbow when you squeeze it, which is awkward.

Some of the better sets have numbers on the regulating screw knob. Mine is numbered from 4 to 16. If you watch what happens when you turn the knob, you will see that at the number 4 mark, the anvil is at its lowest position, which means that the plunger pushes the tooth farther sideways. Bring the anvil up on number 10 or 11 and you will see the anvil rising nearly to the top of its slot. At its highest point of travel, the plunger can bend the tooth sideways only a very limited amount.

The numbers are calibrated to correspond with tooth points-per-inch. If you are setting the teeth of a 5-point crosscut saw, number 5 on the regulating knob puts the anvil low so the tooth can be given plenty of set, which

6

is what you want in a fast-cutting coarse-toothed saw. Change it to 10, and the saw set is just about right for the 10-point saw you would use for finer work.

But to some degree, setting the teeth of any saw is pure guesswork, and the amount depends entirely on your experience and knowledge with wood. As a rough guideline, soft green wood requires the most set, dry soft wood a little less, and hardwood, green or dry, still less. I realize that you are not going to reset the teeth of your saw every time you switch from one wood to another, and you are not likely to own enough saws to tailor one to each type of wood. The thing to aim for is to put just enough set in the teeth so that the saw runs free without pinching in the type of wood you saw the most, and let it go at that.

What happens if you overset, and what can you do about it? The result is that the saw bites off more than it can chew and it starts to wobble, producing a wide kerf and a ragged cut. Luckily, reducing overset is quick and easy.

Just lay the handsaw on its side on a flat surface and *side dress* the teeth. Take a three-cornered file and hold it tipped so that one of its edges bears heavier on the blade than on the teeth. Proceed by taking several passes, the same number on each side, so that the set stays even. I suggest you break both ends off a worn-out file for this purpose; a short file, say about 4" long, works best.

If you find you don't have enough set, it's a simple matter to put more in even after the saw has been sharpened—without dulling it—if you're careful.

Now to set the blade's teeth. I'm going to work on a 10-point saw, so we'll set the regulating knob at 10. Choose a place with decent light, and tuck the handle of your saw under your armpit, teeth up, with the tip away from you. You'll see that every other tooth leans to the right, and the alternate ones to the left, if you're dealing with a saw that has been set before, and you begin with the first tooth that leans to the left nearest the tip. (I'm doing the setless blade Mr. Fickett handed me, so I'm free to choose.) Give your saw set a squeeze, and move along to the second tooth away and keep going that way with

every other one until you reach the handle.

Now turn the saw end-for-end, with the tip under your armpit this time, and repeat the exercise, starting with the first tooth leaning to the left and nearest the handle.

Make sure, to the best of your ability, that you squeeze every tooth with the same pressure, and that the set rests on top of the teeth each time.

That's all there is to it, and the same method applies to all handsaws.

FILING THE CROSSCUT SAW

Filing is the next step. Put your saw in the vise with the tip pointing in either direction, and pull the handle up tight, making certain the blade is clamped in the vise's grip. To prevent chattering, the top of the teeth should protrude no more than about 1/4" higher than the top of the vise; the blade should be absolutely level.

The proper file for a 10-point

The set of saw teeth as viewed end-on—

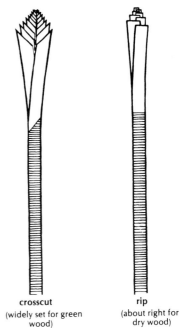

crosscut
(widely set for green wood)

rip
(about right for dry wood)

Setting the teeth of a handsaw—

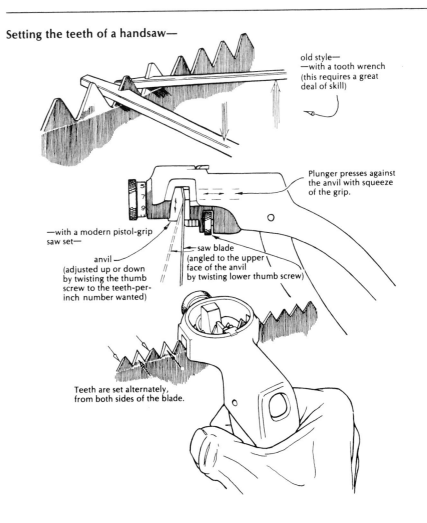

old style—
—with a tooth wrench (this requires a great deal of skill)

Plunger presses against the anvil with squeeze of the grip.

—with a modern pistol-grip saw set—

anvil
(adjusted up or down by twisting the thumb screw to the teeth-per-inch number wanted)

saw blade
(angled to the upper face of the anvil by twisting lower thumb screw)

Teeth are set alternately, from both sides of the blade.

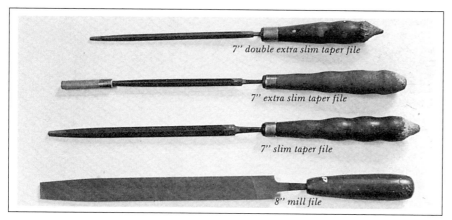

7" double extra slim taper file

7" extra slim taper file

7" slim taper file

8" mill file

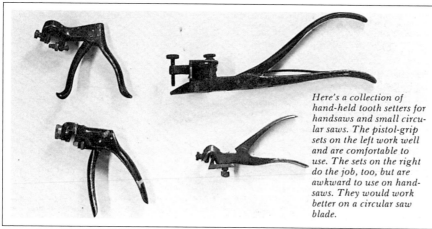

Here's a collection of hand-held tooth setters for handsaws and small circular saws. The pistol-grip sets on the left work well and are comfortable to use. The sets on the right do the job, too, but are awkward to use on handsaws. They would work better on a circular saw blade.

handsaw is a 7" three-cornered double extra slim taper. You could use a smaller one in width and still do a good job, but certainly none larger. To do so invites filing the teeth to oblivion because you can't see what you are doing.

I want to re-emphasize that the first-time filer has a tendency to wobble his way through the filing process, producing rounded-off tooth edges instead of the nice clean chisel edge the filer must always strive for. Part of the wobbling comes from short, poking thrusts guided by an unsure hand. The rest comes from using a file with a handle on one end only. Having handles at both ends not only makes filing more comfortable, it also lengthens the stroke because you don't shorten the cutting action by choking up on the file. I use a wooden handle on the tang end, and for the file's tip I use a 2 1/2" section of a 3/8" dowel, bored to receive it and banded with a brass sleeve sawn from a spent .38-55 cartridge case, which is just about right for fit and keeps the dowel from splitting.

Start filing at the tip of the saw. As I said before, it doesn't matter which way the saw is pointing. Place your file in the groove with the tang handle angled back toward the saw handle as viewed from above, and tilted down about 30 degrees as viewed from the end of the saw. While you're juggling for this position, *think flat* for the top of your file—it should lean neither right nor left.

Eventually you will develop your own style of filing, but this approach works for starters, and it can be varied without ruining cutting quality.

Closely watch the points of the teeth. You are filing two teeth with each pass of the file, and you are taking metal off the face of the tooth leaning away from you and the back of the tooth leaning toward you—I hope in equal amounts. Don't try to get the points sharp the first time around. Instead, bring them nearly to a point the whole length of the blade, then reverse the saw in the vise and repeat the procedure, this time bringing the teeth up sharp. If you point them up

The saw can be put in the vise with its handle in either direction. Natural light is essential, but the lower windowpanes are blocked off so that...

...just the right amount of light is present for accurate filing.

Filing a crosscut saw—

Think "flat" for the top of your file—if peg teeth are wanted.

File-pressure is straight down, although one side or the other may be tailored to regulate the size of adjacent teeth.

file handle depressed about 30°

horizontal

Horizontal, for no-pitch peg teeth. Otherwise, cant the file to produce the pitch wanted.

Tang handle swept back toward the saw handle about 10° for the amount of "fleam" wanted here.

Angling the file into the gullets, from alternate sides, produces pyramidal-pointed teeth with knife edges.

The look of crosscut teeth during the filing process—

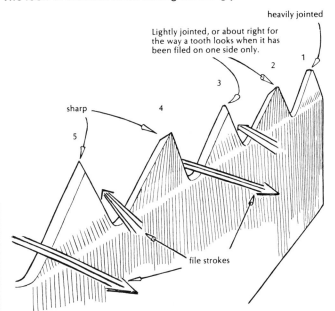

heavily jointed

Lightly jointed, or about right for the way a tooth looks when it has been filed on one side only.

sharp

file strokes

Don't try to get the teeth sharp on the first pass of filing one side. To do so will be to lose your guide—the bright spot of dullness on the point. You'll also cut down the tooth too far to survive the pass of the file on the opposite side.

An experienced saw filer regulates the teeth with tailored short strokes, then does the sharpening with one long stroke per tooth while going down the length of the saw in one pass.

The teeth might look like 2 and 3 at the conclusion of one pass per side. It may require one or two more passes, one long stroke per tooth, to get them looking like 4 and 5.

The saw should be sighted from the ends to be sure that the finished points are the same height on both sides. If not, a further pass on one side will be necessary.

the first time, you are in danger of making them shorter when you hit them again from the other side.

Holding the file as I suggested gives a good tooth shape, with teeth neither leaning ahead nor slanting back very far. When teeth lean ahead too much they grab and chatter; when they slope back too much they simply slide over the wood and cut slowly, if at all. You want the something-in-between that works best for you.

Some saw filers get the correct bevel on their crosscut teeth, but because they hold the file higher than I recommend, they don't get a deep enough gullet between them for chambering sawdust, which is one of the troubles with machine filing.

Whatever style you develop, you will get a saw that cuts free and easy only when its teeth are of uniform height, correctly set and sharp, and when the blade has no kinks.

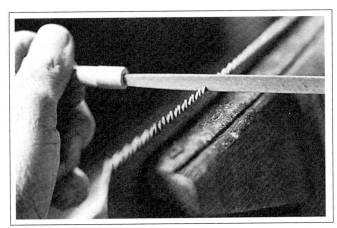

Handles on both ends of the file make it much easier to make the clean, sure strokes that create nice chisel edges.

Notice the sharp teeth on the left side of this saw (about 10 of them) and the dull teeth on the right. The dull teeth shine because their points have just been jointed, but they haven't been filed yet.

CORRECTING PROBLEMS

Let's take a look at a hand crosscut saw that is in all-around bad shape, with large teeth and small, and throw in a kink for good measure.

When you joint the teeth of such a saw, you will see long flat tops on the longer teeth because so much has been taken off them in order to match the heights of the smaller ones. Now it is up to you to get them all back to the same size and height so they will work together again.

Suppose that the saw you just filed ended up with all the short teeth on one side. Then that side can't possibly do its share of the work. Even if you couldn't tell the difference by eye, the unevenness would show up the minute you tried the saw in a piece of wood. That it would cut in a circle like a coping saw should come as no surprise.

Now, as for filing that mess of large and small teeth back into shape, let's see how your hand and eye can accomplish what no machine could ever do. When you find yourself face to face with a long flat top, which is supposed to represent a point but is now maybe more than 1/8" across, here is what you do.

Start with the file in the recommended position and, depending on which way you are facing the saw, exert sideways pressure on the file so that about half the tooth is filed to an imaginary point in the center of the flat area, all the while taking care that you don't hit the already short adjacent tooth.

Let's say you took half of that oversize tooth area off its back side. File all the large teeth the same way and from the same side. Next turn the saw around in the vise and file the fronts of those same teeth, again aiming at the imaginary point. That is how you make them equal in size and evenly spaced again.

REMOVING BURRS

Saw teeth that are already in good shape require only two or three passes of the file to bring them to a point. However, that point you are striving for has a way of hiding behind the burr that forms on the top cutting edge of the tooth leaning away from you.

It's not noticeable on every tooth all the time, but it frequently appears when more pressure than normal is exerted on the file to get the tooth sharp. It can raise havoc with the whole sharpening process unless quickly removed, because you might already have the tooth to a sharp point and not know it and, since the burr looks very much like a dull tooth point, you keep filing away at it until dawn finally breaks and you realize that something is wrong. It certainly is; you're not filing the tooth to a point—in fact, the tooth is almost gone.

Used in time, this is what the wooden handle on your file is for. Just give each tooth a tunk and knock that burr off soon enough so you will be able to see when the tooth comes to a point. That simple trick will keep the beginner from making the most common mistake. Get rid of that burr *before* you think the tooth has reached a point. Then, with just a light pass of the file, bring that tooth all the way up *and no more*. People who notice my chewed file handles often say, "Looks like a beaver's been after them."

While hand and eye are still in the process of becoming really coordinated, there are a couple of other ways to test your expertise besides cutting a piece of wood. Hold your saw with the tip in line with your nose, and you should see a nice even groove down the centerline of the teeth, and you should be able to admire the evenness of their height. Then there's the needle trick I mentioned earlier; people don't

usually believe that the needle can ride the groove between the set teeth right down to the end. My friend Pete Karonis, Cdr., USN (Ret.) didn't. He made me prove it, and was so impressed by the demonstration that he has now taken up the art himself. For the needle to negotiate the trip down the blade, not only must the teeth be reasonably accurate in length and set, the saw must be absolutely free of kinks.

KINKS

Watch an inexperienced worker use a handsaw. He really puts everything he's got into it, he saws fast and bears down hard, and there is nothing smooth or graceful about his act.

Let him strike a spot of poor grain or a hard knot, and when the saw starts to buckle he pushes all the harder. This time the saw really buckles, and he has to stop. He pulls it out and looks at a blade bent into an S curve, curses, throws the saw down, and walks away. None of which would have happened if only he had let the saw do the work while he made long, easy strokes without bearing down. (When the saw started binding, it might have been because the stick was supported by the ends; it isn't always from improperly set teeth.)

Avoid this scenario at all costs, because when you kink a blade, it stretches the metal, sometimes ruining the saw for all time.

In some cases, all is not lost, however. You can remove shallow bends by holding the tip of the saw and the handle and bending the blade back to the opposite curve, overbending, and the blade will pop back straight again.

The worst kinks are the short quick ones. I take them out on a big metal-working vise. You don't get anywhere trying to hammer them flat on an anvil or any other flat surface, because you have to overstretch the metal by the right amount to pop it back. So open the jaws of your vise until they bridge the kinked spot, and hammer lightly, starting around the outside of the kink and working toward its center, closing the vise jaws as you go, so as to match the decreasing size of the kink. Save the last few hammer taps for dead center, using just enough force to cause slight overbend; then finish the spot flat on an anvil.

Before I go on, a word about the 8-

Text continued on page 15

"Regulating" existing teeth—

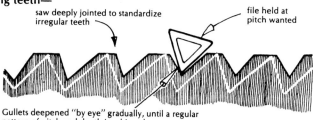

saw deeply jointed to standardize irregular teeth

file held at pitch wanted

Gullets deepened "by eye" gradually, until a regular pattern of pitch and depth is achieved.
File straight across—if major alteration (as this is) is being done.
File diagonally—with the fleam—if regulation to be done is minor.

SETTING UP FOR THE JOB

Just as important as the sharpening technique itself is the means: where you do it, what kind of vise you use to hold the saw, and the sharpening aids you use, such as proper files, saw sets, tooth jointers, raker gauges…on and on the list goes.

As to the where of it, locate your filing vise or vises in front of a window. My own bench is a common plank 9 1/2" wide by 59" long, which is the width of the window. It stands about 40" from its surface to the floor, which would be a bit short for someone taller than my 5'4". One of my two vises is for handsaws, the other for circulars. Both are made of wood, and their tops are chest high, which calls for standup saw filing—just right for the most comfortable filing, as my father used to say. The bench has a coat of flat black paint, and the bottom part of the window is covered with tarred paper to keep out the light and to shut off enough of the window so that, when I am standing at the vise and looking at the teeth, I have a black background.

I've found it advisable to hang a pull shade above the vise so it can be pulled down so the light doesn't strike my eyes but instead strikes the tops of the teeth. Then I can see their shiny tips easily against the black background.

You've probably gathered that I do my saw work only under natural light. Correct. Even when my eyes were younger and I had yet to think of owning a pair of glasses, I never carried out a single step of the saw sharpening process under artificial light. And I don't recommend it now.

The vise I use for handsaws starts with two pieces of oak, 1' tall (the way it is used) by 6" wide and 7/8" thick. Call them parts one and two. They are mirror images of one another. Part one is immovable, screwed into the bench. Both are rabbeted across their tops, 2 1/2" deep by 3/8" wide, to accept the two pieces of oak that actually hold the blade of the saw. These measure 16 1/2" in length and 3" in width and fit snugly into the 3/8" slot of the rabbet, where they are secured by screws. The top edges of these clamping pieces are beveled to 30 degrees, and their ends are tapered to eliminate bluntness.

My bench is notched to the width of 6" to accept part one, and the notch is angled 10 degrees so that the vise leans toward the window by that amount of slope.

The clamping action is activated by a wooden arm about 1' long, rounded at one end and tapered to a handle on the other, which is pivoted on a bolt in the lower right-hand corner of the vise. The rounded end carries a wooden cam, about 5/16" thick and 2" wide. A wooden block, 1 1/8" x 1" x 6" is centered about 6" from the bottom of part one and fastened with bolts through parts one and two; its forward side is rounded, and there is just sufficient play in the through bolts so that the raising of the cam against the curve of the rounded face of this block forces the two top sections of the vise together to hold the saw blade firmly clamped. Strips of sheet lead stapled or tacked to the upper faces of the vise keep the saw from screeching while it is being filed. A brace from the back of the vise to the bench holds the rig firm and solid.

Author's vise for filing handsaws—

16½"

6"

80°

half-round fulcrum

The vise is tilted back 10° to allow a comfortable filing position.

1"

2"

Wooden cam with grain lengthwise

⅜"

1"
1"
2"

12"

4"

Offset pivot brings the cam to bear against the center of the uprights when the handle is horizontal.

Other devices for clamping saws—

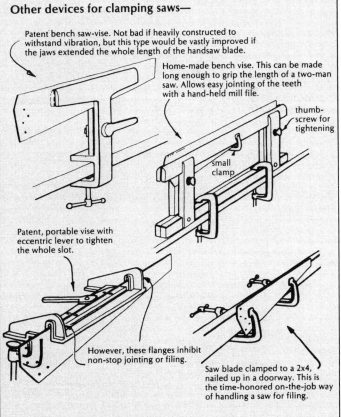

Patent bench saw-vise. Not bad if heavily constructed to withstand vibration, but this type would be vastly improved if the jaws extended the whole length of the handsaw blade.

Home-made bench vise. This can be made long enough to grip the length of a two-man saw. Allows easy jointing of the teeth with a hand-held mill file.

thumb-screw for tightening

small clamp

Patent, portable vise with eccentric lever to tighten the whole slot.

However, these flanges inhibit non-stop jointing or filing.

Saw blade clamped to a 2x4, nailed up in a doorway. This is the time-honored on-the-job way of handling a saw for filing.

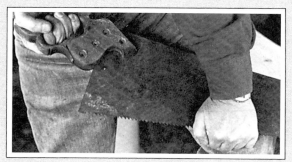

1—The recycling work on this old Disston saw starts with pulling off the old handle.

2—After removing most of the rust with a coarse sanding disc placed in an electric drill, I finish the job with a vibrator sander and 80 grit paper.

3—I used an old saw I was trying to match as a pattern for the new saw and marked the old Disston for recutting. Note the angle of the slot that must be cut in the new handle. The aft end of the old saw is marked for cutting so that it will match.

4—Now the old Disston is marked and ready for cutting.

REJUVENATING AN OLD SAW

Cutting new teeth—

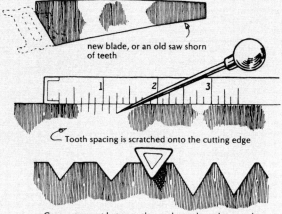

new blade, or an old saw shorn of teeth

Tooth spacing is scratched onto the cutting edge

Grooves are cut between the marks, and are deepened until points are nearly fully formed. Final filing—for fleam and sharpness—will be done after the teeth are set.

There are plenty of good saws floating around out there at flea markets and lawn sales. You won't find many old Disstons—saws possessing a unique quality of hardness that guarantees the best possible cutting edge, and one that stays sharp, filing after filing, long after lesser saws give up—because their owners recognize their worth and are determined to hang onto them. The good old saws you find most often, and occasionally there's a Disston among them, are the old 8-point handsaws, huge things used years ago that fell into disuse when hand-held power saws appeared on the market. The size and awkward handling qualities of the 8-point saws made carpenters not a bit reluctant to hang them up in some obscure corner of the shop, given the handiness of the powered variety.

But the saw you make from one could turn out to be a thing of beauty and a joy forever.

I probably would have never bothered taking the trouble to reclaim one of these relics had I not lost the mate to my favorite old 10-point Atkins. But I thought I could make a better saw out of the old metal than I could buy new over the counter, and I was curious to see if cut-

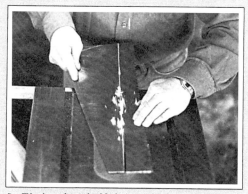

5—The length of the blade is cut freehand and in an unhurried fashion with a cutting wheel on a table saw. I wear a face mask and safety glasses for protection during this part of the job.

ting one of these Goliaths down to size "quick and dirty," the way I planned to do it, would work.

So I went to a lawn sale and came home lugging one of those rusted monsters, with the usual loose handle. It was one of those old-timers with what looked like a gun sight about 4" or so in from the tip. (I, and many others, have wondered about the purpose of this tab for a number of years. Credit for solving the mystery goes to Edward Zanni of Reading, Massachusetts, who has a collection of over 20 Disston handsaws. Zanni says, "The tab was left sticking out perhaps an inch or so by the sawmaker when he made the saw and was used to test the saw's temper during the sawmaking process. It was later broken off, and the distance the tab broke off from the blade told the sawmaker how much or how little temper the blade had.")

There is a big difference between a saw that is a bed of rust, as my new acquisition was, and one that is pitted. If the rust has done its dirty work to the point where you can see roughness etched into the steel, don't bother with it. The teeth will break off when you go to set them. If you're satisfied that the rust is only a thin layer, take your saw home, remove the handle, and take the rust off.

Step one in rust removal is to let your blade soak overnight in a mixture of half water and half white vinegar; my friend Bill Butman, Jr., taught me that trick, and it makes the whole job considerably easier. Then go to work with a power sander—the vibrator type does a fine job.

Next, take your favorite saw and use it as a pattern, assuming you have a favorite. I used the old Atkins I was trying to match in order to replace its missing mate. Put the two saws together, and mark around your pattern saw with a felt-tipped pen or any other medium that will stay there and that you can easily follow while you're cutting the old blade to size. If you don't have a favorite saw, I recommend a straight-backed 10-point saw (that means 10 points to the inch, measuring between the tops of two teeth) with a blade about 20" long for boat work and tight places. I don't like a sway-backed blade; I really don't know why anyone would, since I find it's handy to be able to use my saw as a straightedge.

To cut the old blade down to the traced pattern, put a cutting wheel on your table saw and go to it. I was a little afraid that the heat this generated might ruin the temper of the metal, but it didn't.

Continued on next page.

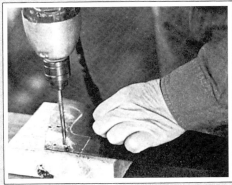

6—Place your new handle pattern on the blade and adjust it to suit for comfort, paying attention to the rake of the hand grip.

7—I ruined almost every drill I had in the shop trying to bore new screw holes in the blade. Next time, I would put the saw blade on a piece of lead and punch the holes out with a machinist's punch of the right size.

8—I used my favorite saw handle as a pattern after tracing it onto the mahogany, and cut it roughly to shape with a bandsaw.

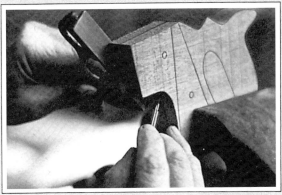

9—Mark the centerline for the blade slot on the new handle, using a tri-square with the rule set to the right depth.

10—Bore two start-holes and use a sabre saw to cut out the grip.

11—Saw the slot for the blade with a backsaw.

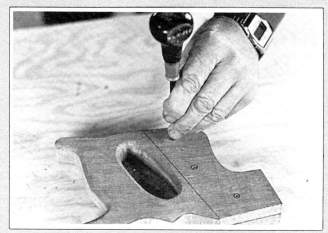

12 — The screw holes for the handle should be prick-punched first to keep the wood bit from wandering while it bores the holes.

13 — Bore or countersink the screw heads and nuts first, then drill for the shanks.

Now that the old 8-pointer has been cut down to size, probably with about 6" off its tip and a couple of inches gone from the bottom of the blade, you have ended up with a nice saw shape but no teeth. It is not beyond human capability to file a new set in by hand, but considering the work and the time involved, I can't really recommend it, not when a machine re-toother can do the job perfectly in 45 seconds. That's right—45 seconds after the machine has been set up, out pops your saw with a brand new and perfect set of teeth.

Leon E. Fickett, who has a saw filing business in Rockland, Maine, did the job for me and charged the sum of one whole dollar. On top of that, because he heard me complaining about the handle that came loosely attached to my bargain saw, he threw in a piece of mahogany robbed from his shop firewood so I could make a new one. So far, not too bad: two bucks for the saw, a dollar for the new teeth, and some handle stock gratis.

I made the new handle by using my favorite saw as a pattern again, tracing the handle on the mahogany. I cut it roughly to shape with my bandsaw and made the grip hole with a sabre saw. With the saw laid flat, I placed the handle on the blade and adjusted it to suit for comfort, paying particular attention to the rake of the hand grip. Then I marked the top and bottom of the blade and drew a line across the handle to show how deep to make the slot to receive it. Screw holes were marked at the same

time, which took all the guesswork out of hitting the holes when I put the handle on.

I used the same saw screws that came out of the original handle, measuring their heads and boring just far enough into the new handle with a bit and brace to recess them. Saw handle screws are two-pieced; you can buy them in almost any good hardware store in case some are missing or you lose them. Because of their male and female fit, you must bore their holes halfway through the handle from opposite sides. Don't forget to bore the recess holes for the heads first, or you are asking for trouble.

The longest part of the job was fitting the handle; that took the better part of a day. I started by sawing the slot for the blade with a panel saw. The table saw was tempting, but I didn't have a blade thin enough to make a snug slot, and I wanted no wobble when that blade was screwed into the handle. I did all this work—the preliminary fitting and the boring of the screw holes—first, before I made any attempt to work up the handle fancy. I've thrown away my share of work by doing the longest and fanciest part of the job first, only to ruin the whole rig by one careless move on the last stroke.

It wouldn't have bothered me if the work had taken twice as long. What's a day or two when you have successfully shaped a discarded old saw into a tool tailored exactly to your needs—one that will last a lifetime?

Moreover, I had learned something.

14 — Use rasps, files, and sandpaper to work the handle down to the smooth shape you want.

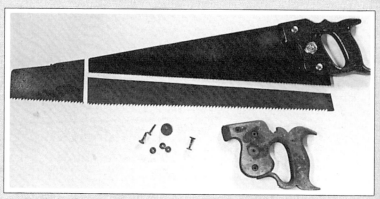

15 — Here's the old saw made new again, and all the leftover pieces.

point crosscut saw. This and a 10-point, perhaps along with a panel saw, are about all you need to do the average carpentry job. Because of the fewer teeth per inch, and therefore larger ones, the 8-point saw cuts faster and a bit rougher. It is good for framing and other heavy work in boat and house carpentry. There is no difference between it and the finer-toothed saw when it comes to sharpening, *except* that you do use a 7" extra slim taper file, which is a little larger than the double extra slim taper.

THE RIPSAW

Since the advent of the Skilsaw, the hand ripsaw has been hung up to gather dust in most shops, including my own. I don't feel the least sorry about it; ripsawing down the length of a board by hand doesn't appeal to me in the slightest, compared to the ease and speed of the Skilsaw.

Still, there are places where power is unavailable, and pushing a ripsaw is tolerable if you're making only a few

Filing a ripsaw—

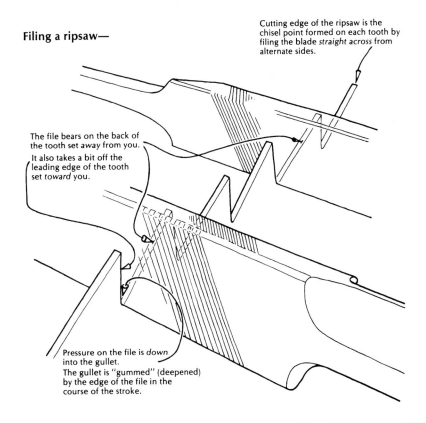

Cutting edge of the ripsaw is the chisel point formed on each tooth by filing the blade *straight across* from alternate sides.

The file bears on the back of the tooth set away from you. It also takes a bit off the leading edge of the tooth set *toward* you.

Pressure on the file is *down* into the gullet. The gullet is "gummed" (deepened) by the edge of the file in the course of the stroke.

THE DISSTON STORY

A stroke of luck brought Bill Disston, great-grandson of Henry Disston, to my shop to pick up a skiff, and I soon raised the question of how the extraordinary temper and hardness without brittleness was achieved in the old Disston blades. Bill now lives in Florida, and he answered me with a letter dated March 4, 1981, which I excerpt here:

Henry Disston was born in England in 1819 and came to the U.S. at the age of 14 with his father, who died three days after their arrival and left him without friends or relatives. He lived with a family in Philadelphia, where he apprenticed himself to a saw firm named Lindley, Johnson and Whitecroft. He worked there for seven years and left to start his own saw company in 1840.

He started making saws in a cellar. By 1855 he was able to move into a building with steam power, where he designed and built a furnace for smelting steel. He developed his own steel "formula" and smelted the first saw steel to be made in the United States. His catalogue of 1855 listed circular saws of 4-60" diameter, segment veneer saws, mill, Tulay, pit, and crosscut saws. It also listed some 20 varieties of hand, panel, rip, half-back bench saws, buck saws, turning webs, compass, pruning, grafting, hack saws, keyhole, and butcher saws, etc. Later, the company made other tools such as plastering and brick-pointing trowels, carpenter's squares, cane knives, bevels, marking and mortising gauges, and still later a complete line of garden and pruning tools. Disston and Nicholson were the only American companies which made a

complete line of files, both American and Swiss patterns.

Disston saw steel was heat-treated in the plant and was harder than competitive saws. We rolled our own saw sheets on a sheet mill so we could control the direction of grain within the sheet, enabling us to set the teeth at that hardness without their breaking. Disston saws were of a hardness that read 52-54 on the Rockwell "C" scale, and competitive saws were 46-48, 10-15% softer than Disston's. They did not know the secret of how to roll a new saw sheet so the teeth would not break during setting at that hardness.

Henry Disston had four sons and the youngest, William, was my grandfather. All four sons were active in the business, but my grandfather was the most active and was president from 1900 until 1915, when he died at the age of 56.

The company was owned and operated by the Disston family until 1955, when it was sold to the H.K. Porter Company of Pittsburgh. From that time on, the company became less prestigious throughout the industrial world as they discontinued a great number of products, mostly in the industrial wood cutting field. The Disston handsaw is still well received, but I believe mostly because of its name rather than its superior cutting quality today.

In 1938 the company developed the first gasoline-driven chainsaw in the United States and supplied them to the Corps of Engineers, which used them exclusively during World War II. During the 1940s, the Disston chainsaw was Number One in the country, but H.K. Porter discontinued its manufacture in 1956.

cuts. I use mine maybe once a year, when I'm forced to make a long cut by hand. For cuts of only a few inches, I use my crosscut rather than take the bother. If I faced a court order to give up one saw, you can bet the hand rip would be it.

With an average tooth count of six per inch, the ripsaw is also a rough cutting tool, but filing it is a little different from working on the crosscut. You file the teeth straight across, 90 degrees to the blade, and you can do all this from the same side of the saw. You use a 7" slim taper file, held so the flat of the file, which touches the forward edge of the tooth, is held at about vertical. Jointing and setting are the same as for the crosscut saw.

SAW FILING GUIDE

Throughout this discussion, I emphasize self-reliance and minimize the use of "helpful" aids. Undoubtedly you will hear of many gadgets, and people

will try to sell them to you. Some you may find useful, others not. Among the latter I include those devices created by some toolmakers solely for the purpose of creating an artificial dependency, one you can well do without.

Depending on the degree of trust you place in yourself, you may find it desirable to adopt one or two devices that I put in a gray category: You really shouldn't need them, but if they help you through the learning stages, why not give them a try? I submit as an example a handsaw filing device marketed by Speed Corporation,

Canby, Oregon 97013. Arnold Joy kindly loaned me one and I tried it out, so I feel competent to comment on its good features and its limitations.

Basically, the saw-filing guide is a hacksaw-like frame with a file in place of a cutting blade. The top is formed of a 1/4" round rod, and on this a circular element holding a file slips back and forth as you work; this rotates as well, providing the opportunity for

Jointing raker teeth by peening—

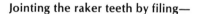

A tack hammer or light riveting hammer is applied to the raker points after the saw has been jointed, set, and sharpened in the usual way.

With the saw held in the vise, bend the point of each raker slightly downward with light taps of a small hammer. The saw metal is malleable enough at the tip of the point to accomplish hooking it downward by 1/64" without breaking it off.

Judge the gaps by means of a straightedge laid across the points of the adjacent cutter teeth.

Jointing the raker teeth by filing—

(1)—A patent raker-tooth jointing gauge may be used, or...

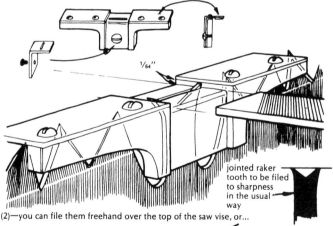

1/64"

jointed raker tooth to be filed to sharpness in the usual way

(2)—you can file them freehand over the top of the saw vise, or...

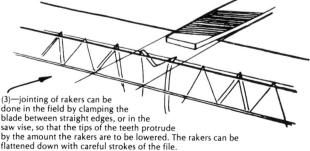

(3)—jointing of rakers can be done in the field by clamping the blade between straight edges, or in the saw vise, so that the tips of the teeth protrude by the amount the rakers are to be lowered. The rakers can be flattened down with careful strokes of the file. The tips are then filed once again to sharpness.

Buck saws—

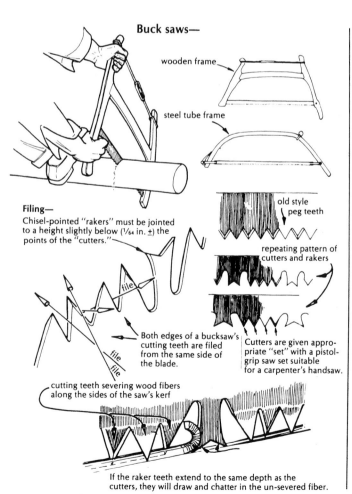

wooden frame

steel tube frame

Filing—
Chisel-pointed "rakers" must be jointed to a height slightly below (1/64 in. ±) the points of the "cutters."

old style peg teeth

repeating pattern of cutters and rakers

Both edges of a bucksaw's cutting teeth are filed from the same side of the blade.

Cutters are given appropriate "set" with a pistol-grip saw set suitable for a carpenter's handsaw.

cutting teeth severing wood fibers along the sides of the saw's kerf

If the raker teeth extend to the same depth as the cutters, they will draw and chatter in the un-severed fiber.

considerable adjustment. Another good feature is that the circular unit can be swung right or left at various angles, and locked in the position you choose. You need only place it on top of the saw's teeth, and a groove along the bottom guides the device along for you. You have to move it along the saw blade each time you pass the file across the teeth, but it does guarantee a precision stroke every time.

My objection to the saw-filing guide is that it slows the work of filing. Also, because the file is locked into position, you can't very well bring side pressure to bear on a tooth that is larger than the rest and needs individual attention. I don't use this tool for the same reason I don't use a power-driven filing machine: It does not permit the exercise of personal judgment; it, not you, controls the operation. Yet I don't condemn it. Learn with it if you like, and keep on using it if you get the results that you seek.

BOW SAW AND BUCK SAW

As far as I can see, the only difference between a bow saw and a buck saw is in the nature of the frame—the bow saw's is of bent metal pipe and the buck saw's is of wood. They're both used for the fast hand cutting of firewood and bigger timbers for which a regular handsaw would be inappropriate. Their blades are under tension so they can be thin and their teeth are coarse. Some of the blades are tempered and are so hard they cannot be filed; all you can do is throw them away when they become dull. The blades made of softer metal can be filed.

Bow and buck saw blades are of two basic types: those with crosscut teeth all of the same pattern, and those with both crosscut and raker teeth. In the latter type, the usual arrangement is four crosscut teeth, a raker tooth, four crosscut teeth, a raker tooth, etc. The crosscut teeth do the slicing and are shaped to cut on both the push and the pull strokes, unlike the hand crosscut, which cuts only on the push stroke. The rakers, or cleaners if you will, simply push the sawdust out of the cut.

Bow and buck saws were used extensively by professional woodsmen years ago, and only gave way on that joyful day when the chainsaw was born. Today they are used only by a handful of people—probably no serious woodcutters, only exercise hobbyists.

Because bow and buck saw blades are so thin, and the metal of the fileable ones is so soft, it is easy to ruin the teeth when filing them. Keep in mind that the cutting teeth bevels are very similar to those of a hand crosscut saw, except that both edges of each tooth are filed for cutting equally well in both directions. Raker teeth are filed straight across, just like those of a rip-

Two-man saws—

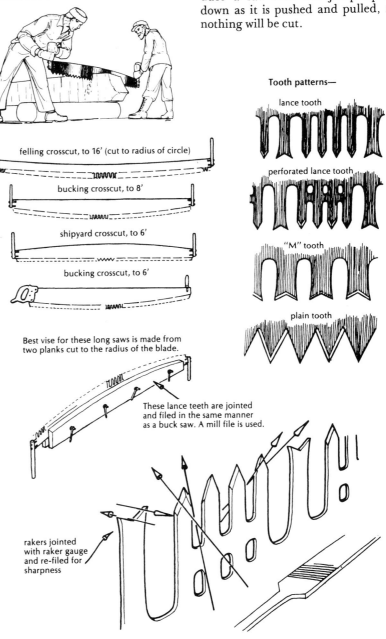

felling crosscut, to 16' (cut to radius of circle)

bucking crosscut, to 8'

shipyard crosscut, to 6'

bucking crosscut, to 6'

Best vise for these long saws is made from two planks cut to the radius of the blade.

These lance teeth are jointed and filed in the same manner as a buck saw. A mill file is used.

rakers jointed with raker gauge and re-filed for sharpness

Tooth patterns—

lance tooth

perforated lance tooth

"M" tooth

plain tooth

saw, and their height is regulated by using a raker gauge.

When filing, joint the teeth first and then set them an amount appropriate to the type of wood being cut. Place the case-hardened raker gauge with its ends resting on the cutting teeth that flank the raker. File the raker point flat across, which will bring it about 1/64" below the adjacent cutting teeth. When you are filing the crosscut teeth, file the rakers to a point, too, but only their points. Failure to file the rakers below the height of the cutting teeth will produce a saw that will jump up and down as it is pushed and pulled, and nothing will be cut.

Setting a two-man crosscut—

(1) with spring-set device—

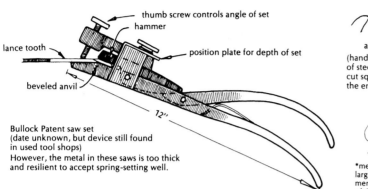

thumb screw controls angle of set

hammer

lance tooth

position plate for depth of set

beveled anvil

12"

Bullock Patent saw set
(date unknown, but device still found
in used tool shops)
However, the metal in these saws is too thick
and resilient to accept spring-setting well.

(2) with hammer and anvil (and skill)*

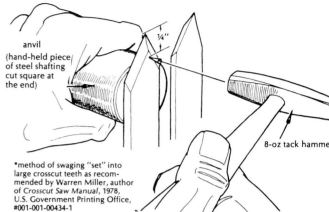

anvil
(hand-held piece
of steel shafting
cut square at
the end)

¼"

8-oz tack hamme

*method of swaging "set" into
large crosscut teeth as recommended by Warren Miller, author
of *Crosscut Saw Manual*, 1978,
U.S. Government Printing Office,
#001-001-00434-1

TWO MAN CROSSCUT SAW

The two-man crosscut saw does the same job as the buck saw, but it is much longer (about 5') and has a much thicker blade that is 5" to 6" in depth. It has both crosscut and raker teeth. Two men who work well together can go through a log with one of these almost as fast as one man with a chainsaw, but the blade must be in tiptop shape. Men have to rest, chain-saws do not, which is the main reason why the two-man saw went the way of the buck saw. Today, it is reserved for lumberjack contests.

Even though the two-man crosscut saw is seldom used, knowing how to make one cut well is one of the arts of saw filing. Because the steel is extra thick, you have to set the cutting teeth with a hammer and anvil. The raker teeth are taken down the same way as the buck saw's, but because the cutting teeth and the rakers are on a larger scale, the difference in their heights is proportionately greater. The correct file for this saw is a 7" or 8" slim taper, or a flat mill file.

I know I haven't been all that encouraging about the use of these monsters, but I will say that back in the mid-1950s, my wife, Amy, and I managed to get through five cords of spruce that Hurricanes Carol and Edna left behind like jackstraws. The quiet swish of the blade, the brush-wood bonfire, the picnic lunches, the pulling together—all these elements out in God's environment combined to give us very pleasant memories.

Two-man crosscut—

Gauging set by use of a "spider"—

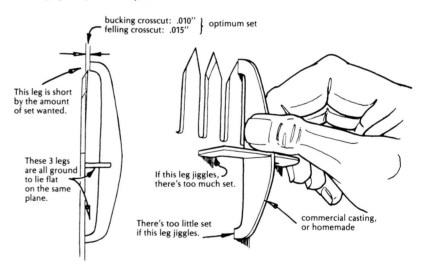

bucking crosscut: .010"
felling crosscut: .015" } optimum set

This leg is short
by the amount
of set wanted.

These 3 legs
are all ground
to lie flat
on the same
plane.

If this leg jiggles,
there's too much set.

There's too little set
if this leg jiggles.

commercial casting,
or homemade

To correct an overset cutter tooth—

1—Tap some of the set out with the hammer.

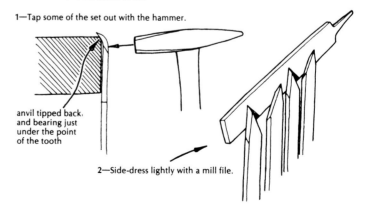

anvil tipped back,
and bearing just
under the point
of the tooth

2—Side-dress lightly with a mill file.

POWER SAWS

"Yes, I could fix it," I told my son Neil when he handed me the worst-looking 8" circular saw I'd ever laid eyes on in my life, "but I won't."

Neil had picked the thing up one day at a bargain price. And no wonder—everything that could be wrong with a saw was wrong with this one.

For starters, one quick glance told me that the saw was out of round, that the teeth lacked even the barest hint of set, and that it had been filed by someone who knew absolutely nothing about the art of filing or the proper shape of teeth. Like most amateurs, he—I suppose nowadays I had better add "or she"—had taken the path of least resistance and filed only the front part of the tooth tops of this coarse-toothed ripsaw, so the after parts of the teeth ended up higher than their cutting edges. At this point the saw gave up, because the backs of the teeth were being asked to do the cutting and they refused the job.

Still undaunted (but none the wiser), the anonymous filer seized on a last-ditch operation: he decided that the saw's woes could be cured by gum-ming the teeth—that is, cutting the gullets deeper between the teeth—so he went at it, gumming away with a square-edged gumming wheel. The wheel was the wrong shape to begin with, and was also too small. Strangely enough, the filer did possess a sense of symmetry when it came to grinding; unfortunately, it was the wrong kind.

This process produced a pattern that aimed the front edge of every other tooth precisely at the center of

"It was the worst-looking saw I'd ever laid eyes on."

the arbor hole, or exactly where the front edge of a ripsaw tooth should not point. By some miracle, the front edges of all the other teeth slanted ahead, at a rake to the midpoint of a radius from the arbor hole to the outside edge, exactly as they should.

Since the day its owner bought that saw, a lot had happened to it, and none of it good. The "sharpening" that turns a perfectly good saw into a useless wreck is not at all untypical. You, too, can do it. Just pick up a file, and go blindly at your saw.

Perhaps you're wondering why I told my son I wouldn't fix his saw for him. My immediate reaction was that it should be kept as a memorial to the worst job of filing imaginable—to fix it would deprive the world of a prime example of just how messed up a saw can get.

But of course I would fix it for him, and I did. However, I wanted to postpone its rejuvenation for a while until I was ready to write this manual. Now you can see this same saw photographed before and after, and it will help you see what I am talking about.

SHARPENING
THE CIRCULAR SAW

I sharpen circular saw blades at the same workbench I use for sharpening handsaws, but I use a vise like the one shown in the drawing. This rig is lead sheathed like my handsaw vise, and is braced so it stands perpendicular to the bench surface instead of being mounted on a slant.

Small circular saws come with a variety of tooth patterns and with different numbers of teeth, from the many-toothed plywood and veneer-cutting saws to the skip-toothed type. Some are designed to cut across the grain, some with the grain, and some to cut both ways. These double-duty combination blades never work as well as a saw designed for one specific cut. Most woodworking shops do a variety of jobs requiring many different cuts, and always have saws matched to specific functions.

There are two styles of circular saw blades that are commonly used for work where speed and production are more important than quality. One is the straight ripsaw, designed for cutting a board along its length, and the other is a combination saw whose blade looks like a rip's but is actually filed slightly differently so it will cut both across and with the grain. It works best when ripping, but can be used for small amounts of crosscut work. These two types are both of the coarse-toothed family, an 8" saw having 20 teeth, more or less, that require setting.

Then there is the veneer or plywood saw, which comes with fine teeth and plenty of them—more than I will take the time to count, let alone file. It is used for work that cannot tolerate any torn or splintered edges, such as trimming the tops and bottoms of mahogany flush doors. I refuse to own one, simply because I don't want to file that many teeth.

Instead, for a fussy job I get the same results with a hollow-ground combination blade, often called a planer blade because of the planed look and feel of its cut. Hollow ground means the blade is thicker at the rim, where the teeth are, then tapers to become thinner toward its center. That configuration keeps the saw from binding; no set is needed to the teeth and every cut looks and feels as if it had been hand planed. This is the Cadillac of saws for shopwork. But it has to be kept sharp and in excellent shape, or it will quickly lie down on the job. Use it only for the top-quality jobs requiring high accuracy, and use it only in dry wood. If I'm using one of these planer blades in plywood, I find that masking tape over the area to be cut keeps splinters to a minimum and yields results that are fully adequate.

The author's vise for sharpening circular saws—

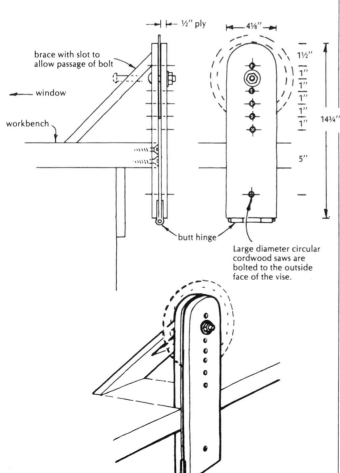

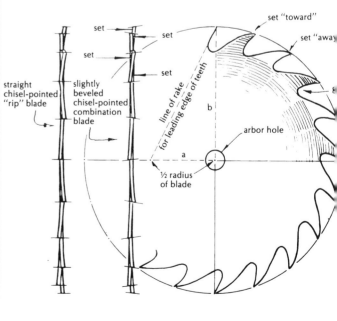

The look of "set" and "half pitch" in a 20-point circular saw for ripping—

RIPSAW BLADE

Let's go back to the straight ripsaw. The word "straight" is my own description, not the manufacturer's. I use it to mean that cutting fast with the grain is the only work I expect this saw to perform. In order for this blade to do its best, it has to be kept round by jointing the teeth.

You can do this on your tablesaw. Crank the saw blade down below the table height, then lay a file over the slot (a flat mill file is best) and crank the blade up again until it just touches the file. Rotate the saw *backward* by hand, using the belt. Do this until all the teeth show they have been hit by the file.

Next comes the set. Sears, Roebuck offers a nifty circular saw set that mounts in the miter slot of a saw table as shown. Using it, Sears says, is "as simple as driving a nail," and it is. My set came in a small cardboard box, which contained four arbor centers ranging from ½" to 1", and Sears threw in a wrench for adjusting the whole setup for different-size miter slots. The rig can be adjusted to any size saw that the tool has the power to set; the punch is spring-loaded and jumps back out of the way for the next tooth to come up for a whack. Anyone who has read my book *Instant Boats* (International Marine Publishing Co., Camden, Maine) knows that I have not been generous with praise for Sears, Roebuck tools, but in all fairness, this one is very good.

If you don't happen to own such a unit, however, and if your circular saw is small—say, below about 12"—you can use your handsaw set, adjusted the same way as for handsaws; that is, smaller numbers mean more set.

Most pure circular saw sets that are hand struck with a hammer have no numbered settings, and using them is pure guesswork based on your own experience and knowledge of the wood to be cut. All are adjustable, though.

To begin the process of setting the saw, mark a tooth with a felt-tipped pen or grease pencil. Looking edge-on at the teeth, note whether they are leaning to the right or the left. Then proceed to set every tooth that leans away from you, which will, of course, be every other tooth. When you come again to the marked tooth, turn the blade over and repeat the operation on the alternate teeth. Setting is done only when there is an obvious lack of it; it's not needed every time the saw is filed.

The teeth I'm talking about here are all regular in size and shape. The saw my son handed me, which I postponed "fixing," had teeth that were anything but. On a saw as loused up as his, the teeth must first be shaped by gumming. Generally speaking, this has to be done by a machine, such as the one built by my father and described later on, or by a professional filer set up for this operation. However, with care and patience you can deepen your saw's gullets—gum the saw, that is—yourself as suggested in the drawing.

For the ripsaw, the leading edge (or front part of the tooth) must slant ahead; that is, it must follow an imaginary line drawn from its point to the midpoint of the horizontal line running from the arbor hole to the outside edge or rim of the blade as shown in the drawing. This assumes that the tooth we are talking about is at the very top of the saw, so a vertical line dropped down from its point will meet the horizontal line at the center of the arbor hole, and the two will form a right angle. The line projected by the leading edge, or followed by it, is the hypotenuse of a right triangle, and its base is half the radius of the saw.

That is called half pitch. If you alter the line of the leading edge so it falls more inboard, nearer the arbor hole, the saw will still cut, but not as fast. Increase the pitch by having the line strike the horizontal nearer to the rim of the saw, and the tooth bites off too much and has a tendency to bang into the wood. It is also more fragile and will dull sooner.

I'm not saying that any deviation from half pitch brings dire consequences—only that this seems to be the most effective pitch for most purposes.

Gumming has to do with the gullet or space between the teeth, which carries the sawdust out of the kerf and clear of the work. There is no hard rule about the depth of the gullet, only that it should be reasonably deep, well-rounded, and strong. By *strong* I mean that the back of the tooth should

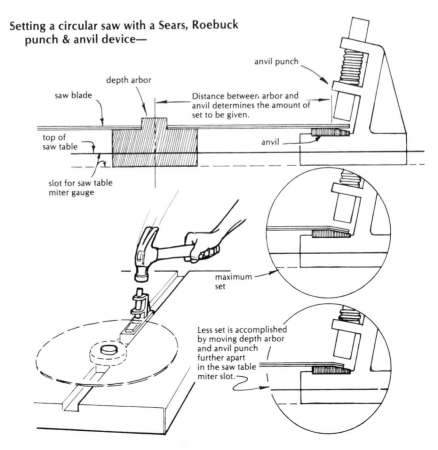

Setting a circular saw with a Sears, Roebuck punch & anvil device—

anvil punch

depth arbor

saw blade

Distance between arbor and anvil determines the amount of set to be given.

top of saw table

anvil

slot for saw table miter gauge

maximum set

Less set is accomplished by moving depth arbor and anvil punch further apart in the saw table miter slot.

Rip blade—

With chisel-pointed teeth
for along-the-grain raking—

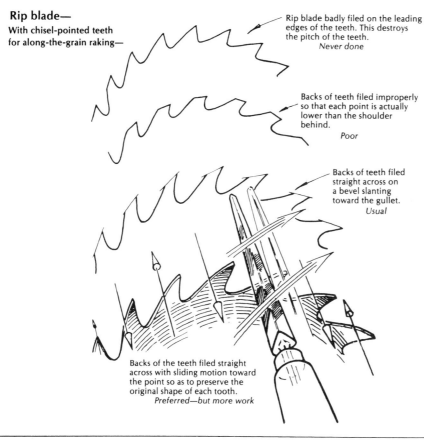

Rip blade badly filed on the leading
edges of the teeth. This destroys
the pitch of the teeth.
Never done

Backs of teeth filed improperly
so that each point is actually
lower than the shoulder
behind.
Poor

Backs of teeth filed
straight across on
a bevel slanting
toward the gullet.
Usual

Backs of the teeth filed straight
across with sliding motion toward
the point so as to preserve the
original shape of each tooth.
Preferred—but more work

"Gumming"— Deepening the gullet—

bench-mounted, motor-driven abrasive wheel

saw blade repositioned
for each bite of the abrasive
wheel

shallow gullets
between sharpened-down
old teeth

blade bolted to
a positioning plate

Properly shaped abrasive wheel
powered by table saw arbor, or
by a hand-held electric drill, or
perhaps by the H.W. Payson Gumming &
Sharpening Machine. A selection of
gumming wheels should be kept on hand
for saws of various tooth sizes.

Gullets may be deepened by
skillful use of a ⅜" rat-tail file.

deepened gullets with
properly rounded bottoms

Shape of the tooth
may be altered to suit—
with the gumming
wheel, or by file,
afterwards.

sweep up from the gullet in a grace-ful curve until it meets the point. Sure, with successive jointings and fil-ings the gullet gradually becomes smaller and the shape of the back of the tooth changes, but as long as you leave the front part (the gullet side) alone and don't file it, then the lead-ing edge will retain its shape until the saw needs gumming again.

As you file the teeth and the saw wears down, keep the upper part of the tooth's back in mind, too. There's an easy rule to remember here, and it involves another imaginary line—one running from the point of the tooth to halfway between the gullet and the top of the next tooth. Keep the back of the tooth filed to that imaginary line, and the saw will never hang up because the backs of its teeth are higher than the points.

By starting to file at the back of the tooth and bringing the tooth up to a point with a sliding motion (yes, I know it's more work), you will main-tain that perfect blend of angles between the top and the leading edge of the tooth that produces the best cut-ting action. Don't file the gummed or leading edge unless it gets damaged, no matter what you see or hear. Always remember that for a ripping blade, that edge needs to be square—just the same as with the hand rip-saws—and to the correct pitch. File it, and you are in danger of slanting the tooth back and destroying the cutting qualities.

In a reputable tool manufacturer's catalog I recently came across a listing for a sharpening device strapped to a circular ripsaw, with the file passing across the gummed leading edge of the tooth—exactly what I have just fin-ished bitching about. The illustration also shows a file angle adjustment device—which you don't need for a ripsaw. All you need to do to file the coarse-toothed ripsaw is to file the tooth tops straight across with a 7" slim taper file.

I've read at least two manuals on saw filing that told me that teeth are filed against their set instead of with it. Not in this manual, and not in my shop, either.

In the first place, filing against the set puts the filer in an extremely awkward position, for in order to get any depth at all to the gullets, you would have to hold your elbows in an elevated (and very tiring) position. Worse still, going against the set like that means filing the face of the tooth leaning toward you, which guarantees there will be slivers of steel flying through the air in your direction. Working that way without glasses is asking for trouble. Not only is that method hazardous, it just doesn't seem natural, and your file tells you so as it chatters its way across the tooth. The only reason I can see for such an approach is that it eliminates the burr on the tooth's point that you get when filing with the set. But that's taken care of by a *tunk* with your wooden file handle, as I explained on p. 10 of this manual.

COMBINATION BLADE

If you put a straight ripsaw and a combination saw side by side in profile and look at them, you can't tell the difference between them. They may have the same number of teeth and look identical, but in fact the teeth of the combination blade have a slight bevel on their tops—somewhere between 5 and 12 degrees (see drawing). That small bevel is what allows you to saw across the wood's grain as well as with it, though not quite as well in either case as with the pure rip or the pure crosscut. To get the bevel, tip the handle of the file down anywhere from 5 to 12 degrees instead of filing straight across the top of the tooth with the file dead flat level. There's nothing fussy about it.

If you find that you have put too much set in the teeth of the straight ripsaw or the combination blade, you can easily remove the excess set by

Taking out the excess set on an abrasive wheel.

Combination blade—
—with slightly beveled, pointed teeth for ripping or crosscutting—

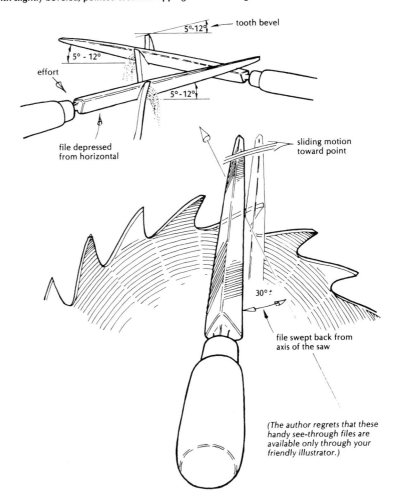

tooth bevel

5°-12°

5° - 12°

effort

5°-12°

file depressed from horizontal

sliding motion toward point

30°±

file swept back from axis of the saw

(The author regrets that these handy see-through files are available only through your friendly illustrator.)

laying the blade, first on one side and then the other, on a larger diameter abrasive cutting wheel and rotating the blade backward by hand. Rub both sides with the same number of passes. This is good practice anyway on a circular saw that has been hand set, because a spring-set tooth doesn't have the accuracy the hammer and anvil method can produce. Just a light, smooth rubbing evens the set for a smoother cut.

HOLLOWGROUND PLANER BLADE

Sometimes called the "smooth-cut combination blade," the hollow-ground planer blade is difficult to file in terms of accuracy, and accuracy is a must if you are to get the smoothness of cut you expect from the saw. The source of that smoothness is the hollow-ground blade, with its greatest

thickness at the rim, tapering to become thinner toward the center. Because the rim is thicker than the center part, it clears its own path without set in the teeth, and the absence of set makes it cut smoothly. There is little side friction as long as you use the saw for what it is designed to do—to cut dry, seasoned wood, not green 2 x 4s.

But suppose you want to benefit from the saw's smooth cutting action, and the wood you'd like to use it on has a bit of moisture in it? In that case, put just a little set in the teeth—and I mean *little*. There will be some loss of smoothness when you make the cut, but the results are better than if you used a rip or combination blade. I use two hollow-ground planer blades, one with just a dite of set and one without.

The planer blade has a repeating pattern of four cutoff teeth for cross-cut work and one raker for ripping teeth are beveled about the same as those of a hand crosscut saw, except the front cutting edge forms a line from the tooth point directly to the center of the arbor hole, resulting in what is called *center pitch*. Power saws have the muscle to push such teeth through the wood, but you don't—which is why the handsaw crosscut teeth must lean back as I have specified.

The raker teeth cut just as the teeth of the straight ripsaw do and are filed the same way, straight across the top, but must be filed lower than the cutting teeth by 1/64" to do their job. How can you tell what 1/64" less is? You can't, unless you have a machine like my father's Rube Goldberg device, which joints each tooth separately (see sidebar). You have two alternatives. You can take the blade to a *competent* professional sharpener, or you can do a pretty fair job yourself if you do the following:

First, joint the blade down so that it is truly round. That makes the

teeth—rakers and all—the same height. Then just file the rakers down slightly beyond the point of sharpness, and you will at least be close. Take the trouble of jointing the saw down lightly like this before sharpening, to keep the teeth as even as possible.

The fronts of the rakers have deep gullets that are shaped like the teeth on straight ripsaws, which have half pitch, you'll remember. Maintain that gullet shape the same way I described earlier.

The only other thing you need to know about filing the planer blade is that the back slopes of adjoining crosscut teeth are beveled automatically when you file their faces by holding your file in a horizontal position with the handle swept back about 30 degrees, as you would with a crosscut handsaw. The backs of the teeth get beveled this way as well as the fronts, though not as much. Remember that you file the smaller saws with a 7" *extra* slim taper, and the larger ones with the slim taper file.

Dado set—

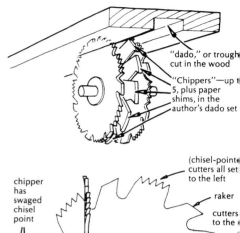

"dado," or trough cut in the wood

"Chippers"—up 5, plus paper shims, in the author's dado set

(chisel-point cutters all set to the left

chipper has swaged chisel point

raker

cutters to the

Combination blade with repeating pattern of rakers and cutters—

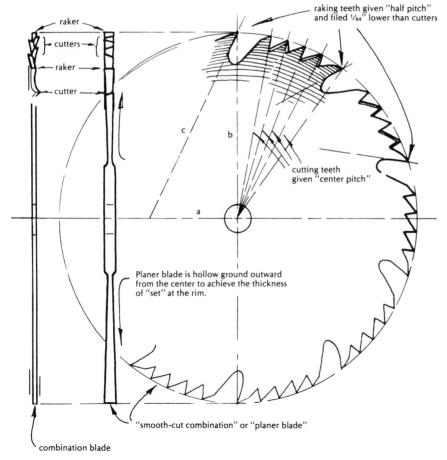

raker

cutters

raker

cutter

raking teeth given "half pitch" and filed 1/64" lower than cutters

cutting teeth given "center pitch"

Planer blade is hollow ground outward from the center to achieve the thickness of "set" at the rim.

"smooth-cut combination" or "planer blade"

combination blade

DADO SETS

Dado sets come with two blades that look very much like the hollow-ground planer blade, but with a different tooth pattern. These blades have a group of cutting teeth with one raker per group. Unlike the teeth of the planer blade, all five cutoff teeth in each group are set in the same direction and are filed alike. Alternate groups are set in the alternate direction. The rakers are much bigger and stronger, and are gummed slightly more toward center pitch than half pitch. The blades are held apart by chippers—five in the set I have—which are somewhat like two triangles joined together with a raker at each point. These chippers are used in combination with paper washers as spacers to make a cut of any width within the set's capabilities.

A dado set is nice to have if you are going to do a lot of precision work requiring grooves and rabbets, but it is hardly necessary for only occasional work. You can handle that with your tablesaw in just a few cuts, simply by moving your rip fence over by the width of the blade after each cut.

CORDWOOD SAW

The big old cordwood saw holds a special meaning for me. Every winter when I was a kid, my father and I hopped aboard our old Model T cut down for a tractor and wound our way over humps and bumps deep into the center of the woodlot. There we felled trees with axe and buck saw all day long. Then we would mount the tractor again and follow the same bumpy road back home, repeating the trip until our sizeable backyard was filled with long lengths of firewood.

Hooked to another Model T engine by a belt, the cordwood saw sang its song daily until the firewood was fitted for the stove. Those were the days of the Great Depression when our country was suffering, but from a kid's point of view the chug of that old engine and the whine of the saw as it sliced its way through stick after stick told my ears that all was right with the world. I'm still fascinated with the saws and the sounds they make. To work with one and hear its music again is always a special delight.

Saws of that size are no toys; they deserve the greatest respect and care. The old-timers were very much aware of that, but occasionally even one of their number would grow a little lax through long familiarity. Before we go further, let me tell you a story about one of those old-timers. He has gone to his reward now; his saw didn't take him, but it came close.

He was Archie H. Rackliff—boat-builder, fisherman, father-in-law, and friend. Archie's wood saw rig was driven by a big stationary engine. As his daughter, my wife Amy, tells it, he always sawed his firewood in one place, never moving it and never completely removing the mound of sawdust that built up around it, either.

One day the blade embedded itself in a big stick of wood and stuck there, pinched for lack of sufficient set. The old engine didn't care. Not even noticeably slowing, it ripped the saw table from its base and threw saw, stick, and all straight at Archie, slamming him in the face and knocking him to the ground. Fortunately the wood stayed stuck on the blade, and though it hit him with enough force to gash his head so that many stitches were required to close the wound, the saw only rolled him down.

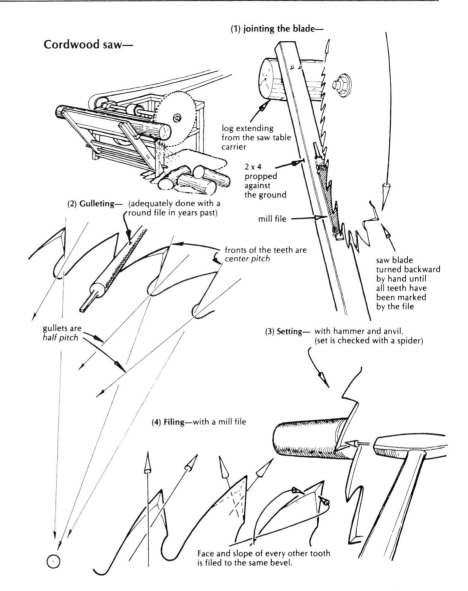

Cordwood saw—

(1) jointing the blade—

log extending from the saw table carrier

2 x 4 propped against the ground

mill file

saw blade turned backward by hand until all teeth have been marked by the file

(2) Gulleting— (adequately done with a round file in years past)

fronts of the teeth are center pitch

gullets are half pitch

(3) Setting— with hammer and anvil. (set is checked with a spider)

(4) Filing—with a mill file

Face and slope of every other tooth is filed to the same bevel.

After that, Archie built a cement foundation for the rig, and never allowed sawdust to accumulate around it. He took care to put some set in the saw's teeth, too.

With that cautionary tale behind us, let's go back to the sharpening of cordwood saws. The tooth gullets of these saws are broad and deep, and are ground to half pitch, but the slope or rake is not brought clear up to the point as with a ripsaw. Just how much face the front of the cutoff teeth must have depends on the size of the saw, but a safe rule is to have a face that is about one third, perhaps slightly more, of the distance from the tooth's point to the gullet. This will ensure a good, strong tooth.

The face and back slope of every other tooth is filed to the same bevel, which can be varied to suit. The greater the bevel, the faster the cutting, but the faster the dulling, too, for a greater bevel makes the tooth point more fragile. Audel's *Carpenters and Builders Guide* says: "Large cutoff saws for cutting large logs, where power feed is used and rapid work is required, should have the pitch line from four to eight inches in front of the center of the saw for softwood, and for hardwood a trifle more hook is preferable."

In my language, this means that the tooth face must slant back slightly (in the opposite way from, say, a ripsaw), so a line projected from it would strike the horizontal radius of the saw at a distance of between 4" and 8" from the center of the arbor. Experience tells me that back slant is easily obtained by the lazy practice of filing just points rather than the whole

THE H.W. PAYSON
GUMMING AND SHARPENING MACHINE

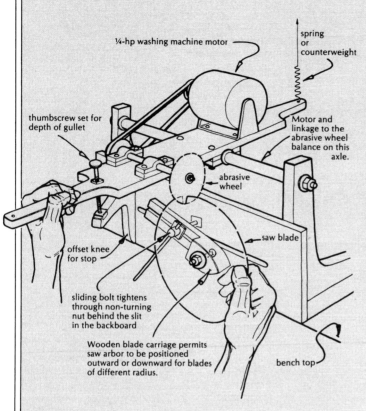

¼-hp washing machine motor

spring or counterweight

thumbscrew set for depth of gullet

Motor and linkage to the abrasive wheel balance on this axle.

abrasive wheel

saw blade

offset knee for stop

sliding bolt tightens through non-turning nut behind the slit in the backboard

Wooden blade carriage permits saw arbor to be positioned outward or downward for blades of different radius.

bench top

I am aware that few readers will want to replicate this machine, even if they are capable of it, for not many need to deal with the wide range of saw sizes it was designed to serve. What I want to do here is explain its principles and some of its chief features. Father said, "I knew what I wanted it to do, and I just built it out of my head as I went along," digging out parts from the depths of his extraordinary junk box.

The power source is a 1/4-hp electric motor taken from a washing machine, and the motor's principal function is to drive a grinding wheel. (Actually, I am using the term "grinding wheel" loosely here. Grinding wheels have square edges and are no good for gumming, because you would get square gullets. Gumming wheels have a rounded cutting edge.) All the elements of the machine are contrived to bring this wheel to bear on shaping the teeth and refining the gullets between them. These pivot on a horizontal 1/2" steel rod, 2' long, which allows the wheel to be lifted up and over a completed tooth and applied to the next one. A combination of slots and the action of an adjustment arm and an adjusting screw make it possible for the machine to accept virtually any size saw, and to direct the cutting edge of the grinder so it will make the appropriate cuts at the angles required for either half pitch or center pitch, as appropriate.

To take one example, this rig greatly simplifies the jointing of a hollow-ground planer blade. All you need to do is joint down all the teeth first, and then, by backing the adjusting screw exactly one turn, the grinding wheel is low-

My father, H.W. Payson, was a professional saw sharpener. He designed a machine for jointing and gumming circular saws and built it from scratch, using parts out of his junk box. I'm still using that machine today and find that from the smallest circular saw to the biggest cordwood saw, it brings them all back with a simplicity of adjustment and a versatility unmatched by any manufacturer's machine I know of. It cannot be beaten, and I can't do without it.

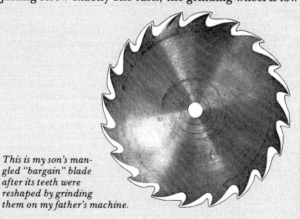

This is my son's mangled "bargain" blade after its teeth were reshaped by grinding them on my father's machine.

face of the tooth, so I shape a newly sharpened saw for center pitch. After you file away at the teeth for a while, you'll see them slant back only too fast and too much. Filing tooth bevels on these big cordwood saws by hand is a real chore; it is best to use an 8" or 9" mill file for this work.

Some words of warning: Beware of heat buildup. Don't try to shape or gum the teeth all at one crack. To do so is to invite excessive heat, which will turn the metal blue and render it too hard to file after it cools. Work your way around the saw, taking off a little at a time. But I have the cart before

the horse. Here, as with any saw, follow the classic order: joint, gum, and shape the teeth; then set and file them.

Don't even try to spring-set the teeth on these cordwood saws. You have to set them with a hammer and anvil. Bill Grierson and I tried to set one of these blades with a big saw set from one of the leading manufacturers, but it just wouldn't do the job. The striking pin was much too small and the bevel much too quick—just right to produce a damaged tooth with no appreciable set.

One variation you may run into on

these cordwood saws is the swaged teeth found on ripping blades. The teeth are not set right and left, but are widened at their points by an equal amount on both sides to widen the kerf for blade clearance.

You do your swaging with a small metal hand tool with a groove in it; place the tool on the point of the tooth and give it enough whacks with a hammer to make the tooth spread out. I would joint those teeth down in the usual way, then swage them, and perhaps joint them again, lightly, before doing any filing. Audel's gives these instructions:

For jointing all kinds of saw teeth, from the raker teeth on a combination blade...

...to the cutting teeth of a cordwood saw,...

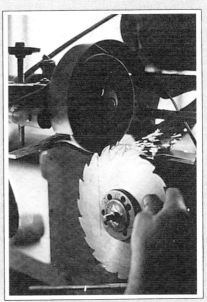

...and for reshaping teeth of an old saw, this machine can't be beat.

red just the right amount to take 1/64" off each raker; lifting the operating handle raises the gumming wheel safely clear of the cutting teeth and ready to hit the next raker when you let it descend again.

Besides accurately jointing teeth, my father's machine can ease the job of filing and at the same time make the saw cut better. It can use a cutting wheel of small diameter and about 3/32" thick to gum out a gullet between each two cutoff teeth on the hollow-ground planer blade. These gullets are raked half pitch, same as for the raker teeth, and are ground just deep enough to chamber sawdust and still keep a strong tooth.

These two examples hardly scratch the surface of the versatility of the H.W. Payson Gumming and Tooth Shaping Machine. Or its accuracy, either. For in the hands of a competent operator, it can never cut at an incorrect angle, nor can it cut any deeper than the limit of the job desired.

If you give the accompanying photos a good, hard look, you will have a better idea of how the machine does what it does. Any verbal description tends to blur into a bewildering recital of dimensions, hole sizes, and the like. Note, for instance, the grayish blob resting in a notch in the wooden arm. That is a heavy lead weight that holds the mechanism firmly in place while it is being used for jointing; remove the weight, and the arm is free to pivot on the rod it's mounted on.

With the lead weight removed, the machine is counterbalanced with a screen-door spring attached to the end of the motor mount. The gumming wheel is then used freehand. In this operation the desired tooth shape (marked on the blade from a paper pattern) comes from using both hands: one to raise and lower the cutting wheel and the other to turn the saw blade into the wheel the right amount so as to grind away the unwanted metal.

Total adjustability: that's the name of the game.

"To swage set a saw:

(1) Make it round by holding a piece of grindstone or soft emery against the rim as it revolves.

(2) File all teeth to a keen point.

(3) Swage from under or top side according to the swage used, 1/16" on each side of the tooth.

(4) Joint again and file square across, or grind to a keen edge without changing the hook.

(5) Side file to bring all teeth to a uniform width. Sharpen saws from two to four times in a full day's sawing."

MILL SAW

Mill saws are the really big ones that turn trees into boards at the sawmill. Sharpening them is a separate art, as is their maintenance. I have little to offer on this subject; I discuss these saws only for the record.

Mill saws are equipped with "insert teeth," which fit into grooves on the blade. The teeth are sharpened by hand, but they are not jointed, gummed, shaped, or set. When the blade needs any of the latter four operations, the teeth are simply replaced.

Great skill is required to keep a mill saw running true without wobbling, which is costly to a mill—oversize kerfs and wasted wood have a way of draining profits. This is where the art of saw hammering comes in. A professional knows just where to strike the blade, and just how hard, to change the rim tension and reduce wobble. The blade is made slightly saucer-shaped.

Bill Grierson knows these saws intimately. A man of many accomplishments and monumental modesty, he built his own sawmill many years ago, and at the age of 70 he is still turning out boards. He tells me that you have to watch these saws constantly. The instant they start binding they will overheat, and then they will start to wobble. If these warnings are ignored, heat buildup will cause a "bull's-eye"—which in sawyer's language means that the saw is unusable, awaiting the attention of a saw hammerer. Sawyers watch for the signs and slack the workload immediately when a bull's-eye occurs, letting the saw run free until it cools again.

The same thing happens to smaller saws on a lesser scale, but they are not worth taking to the professional hammerer.

Mill saw equipped with "insert teeth"—

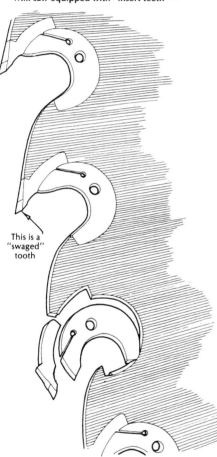

This is a "swaged" tooth

These teeth are file-sharpened and are sometimes side-dressed for specific cutting.
Jointing, gumming, shaping, and setting are accomplished simply by replacing the teeth.

BANDSAW

A bandsaw gets plenty of use in the boatshop; I use mine almost daily. You don't need a large one for build-ing small boats. Mine is a 10" saw, which is the widest cut that can be made between the blade and the frame and is called the throat cut. That 10" limit in width doesn't bother me, because with the right kind of blade—the tempered skip-toothed kind—it will easily slice through 3" and 4" oak, either dry or green.

However, if I get another bandsaw, it most certainly will be larger because the small radius of the drive wheels causes frequent blade breakage. (It would help if I remembered to slack the blade tension between uses.)

If it were not for the tempered blades, this machine would be useless for anything other than thin softwood or plywood; the untempered blades, despite their many teeth, are just not up to doing heavy work. The tempered ones are not yet so expensive that you should spend additional money taking them to a professional shop for sharpening, but you don't have to throw them away when they get dull, either. You can extend their life by sharpening them with a cutting wheel, freehand.

I sharpen mine as many as three times, although the method is far from precise. All it amounts to is touching the back slopes of the teeth with the edge of the cutting wheel spun by a small electric motor. After a few times the teeth become smaller and lose their set (the metal is too hard to stand resetting), they get badly out of shape, or the blade breaks from fatigue. When any one of these things hap-pens, it's time to throw the blade away.

CHAINSAW

I'll admit that for a long time I was leery about chainsaws. I never owned one until cutting wood to heat my house and shop became a serious mat-ter. Chainsaws are dangerous, but you need not fear them as long as you observe some important rules. Here are mine:

The most important is to keep a firm grip on the machine and don't let your mind wander for even a fraction of a second, which is all the time disas-ter takes. The rest require the employ-ment of plain common sense: Wear a hard hat, steel-toed shoes, safety gog-gles, and gloves. Learn which way to fell a tree, how to make the notching and felling cuts and the direction in which to make them. Make sure you have an unobstructed escape route in the far-from-unlikely event that the tree has a mind of its own. With a chainsaw, you learn a little at a time, until the day comes when, without shaking in your shoes, you can waltz up to a tree and lay it down exactly where you want it.

My chainsaw is a Homelite Super 2. It is in the medium-size range, but it is big enough, with its 14" bar, to cut a tree of that diameter—or larger if I work from both sides—and light enough so I can use it all day without tiring.

Chainsaw cutting teeth work on the same principle as those of the hand crosscut saw—they are designed to cut across the grain. How much the teeth hook forward or slant back, as well as how much bevel there is on the cutting edge, determines the speed of cutting.

Unlike the handsaw, chainsaw teeth are neither jointed nor set. You only file across them horizontally with an untapered round file, with its handle raked back about 35 degrees to achieve the proper bevel. No special vise is needed; I use my machinist's vise, after tightening the chain on the guide bar to eliminate wobble. The teeth must be tight enough on the bar so they won't move sideways under the file.

To begin, pick a tooth in the center of the bar that has its bevel facing away from you, and tag it with a felt-tipped pen or grease pencil so you'll know where to stop. Cant your file handle back toward the engine about 35 degrees and file across the tooth with the file parallel to the ground. Pull the chain along carefully so every other tooth comes to the cen-ter of the bar where it can be easily filed. Continue filing every other tooth until you meet the marked one. Reverse the saw in the vise and repeat the process on the alternating teeth.

Saw teeth that have hit a rock need special attention, because the outside top edge of each tooth always becomes rounded over, a condition that effec-tively spoils the chisel effect of the tooth even though it looks and feels sharp after filing. You may be sure that unless the tooth is filed until the rounded portion is gone, your saw will not cut to its full potential. Yet filing the teeth more on one side than on the

Sharpening chainsaws—

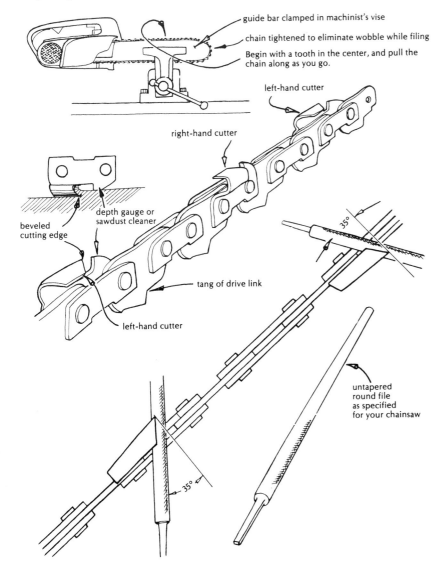

guide bar clamped in machinist's vise

chain tightened to eliminate wobble while filing

Begin with a tooth in the center, and pull the chain along as you go.

left-hand cutter

right-hand cutter

beveled cutting edge

depth gauge or sawdust cleaner

tang of drive link

left-hand cutter

untapered round file as specified for your chainsaw

35°

35°

other will cause the saw to veer off when cutting. For this reason, I strongly recommend that you take all possible care to avoid hitting a rock with your saw.

But in the event that you do hit a rock, careful filing can restore the teeth. Too sharp an angle on the cutting edge will make the tooth grab more wood than it can chew, and it will chatter and dull quickly. If you file too much toward the tip of the tooth, the angle will be too blunt. The teeth will merely slide over the wood, just as handsaw teeth with insufficient rake will.

I can't recommend file sizes to use on your chainsaw, because each model differs. The saw's manufacturer recommends the right size for his models, and the hardware store clerk is supposed to know, but you can't depend on it. I was supposedly given the right size file when I bought my machine, but I was given a larger one when I went back for a replacement. (At about 20 bucks per crack, repair shops love to throw on a new chain to replace one that shows very little wear. This time the retail clerk's mistake was in my favor. With the smaller file I was able to file the teeth to near oblivion and still maintain the hook needed for good cutting.) Use your eyes and your head. If the diameter of your file is too great, you will flatten out the necessary hook in the teeth; if it's too small, you will file too much hook into them.

A properly cutting chainsaw running at full throttle delivers a stream of coarse sawdust at a rate that will bury your shoes out of sight in a hurry.

HUMAN ERROR

No matter how successful we may be in getting our tools in proper shape, there is always the possibility that we might commit colossal blunders in using them. Such errors can result from having done a certain job so often that you no longer think about what you are doing.

I was working on Spruce Head Island one day, ripping boards and 2x4s by portable circular saw. Along with the ripping blade I was using in the saw, I had another blade with me; I don't remember what kind. When it came time for lunch, a summer vacationer staying at the cottage where I was working remarked how well my saw cut—and asked could he use it while I was at lunch. "Sure," I said, and off I went.

When I got back the visitor pointed at a 2x4 he had ripped and said, "That saw of yours didn't work worth a damn." The crooked, burned path he'd made bore him out.

But a look at the saw told me he had changed blades while I was gone, and had installed the new one backward. Yes—he had actually sawed the whole length of that stick with the teeth turning backward! But I said nary a word to him, because I had done the same thing myself, and more than once, though it never took me the length of a 2x4 to recognize my mistake.

At least, errors like this tend to keep us suitably humble.

Filing chainsaw teeth—

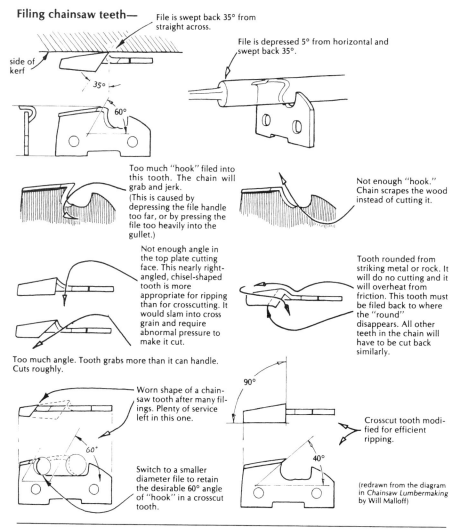

File is swept back 35° from straight across.

File is depressed 5° from horizontal and swept back 35°.

side of kerf

35°

60°

Too much "hook" filed into this tooth. The chain will grab and jerk.
(This is caused by depressing the file handle too far, or by pressing the file too heavily into the gullet.)

Not enough "hook." Chain scrapes the wood instead of cutting it.

Not enough angle in the top plate cutting face. This nearly right-angled, chisel-shaped tooth is more appropriate for ripping than for crosscutting. It would slam into cross grain and require abnormal pressure to make it cut.

Tooth rounded from striking metal or rock. It will do no cutting and it will overheat from friction. This tooth must be filed back to where the "round" disappears. All other teeth in the chain will have to be cut back similarly.

Too much angle. Tooth grabs more than it can handle. Cuts roughly.

Worn shape of a chain-saw tooth after many filings. Plenty of service left in this one.

90°

Crosscut tooth modified for efficient ripping.

60°

Switch to a smaller diameter file to retain the desirable 60° angle of "hook" in a crosscut tooth.

40°

(redrawn from the diagram in *Chainsaw Lumbermaking* by Will Malloff)

Reach down and grab a handful. Roll the grains around in your palm; feel their sharpness and note their size. Use that same perfectly cutting saw without paying attention to the rakers, and you will discover that, despite careful sharpening after each use, as time goes by, the saw won't do its job.

Your feet won't be buried quite so quickly. When you roll the new crop of sawdust in your hand, the individual grains will feel smooth and dull, and they will be much smaller. This change will come about over such a long period of time that you may think you have lost your touch, when actually it is the fault of the saw. Blame it on the clearers, as I call the raker teeth, because they will be too high in relationship to the cutting teeth, which will have diminished in height because of all that sharpening.

Chainsaw clearers perform the same function as buck-saw rakers. My owner's manual calls them "depth gauges," and their heights are governed by a depth-gauge tool. If these clearers or "gauges" are too high, the teeth will not get enough bite, and the result will be slow cutting and fine sawdust. If the clearers are too low (and this doesn't happen by itself), the teeth will bite off too much and will chatter and jump.

Buy a depth-gauge tool to go with your chainsaw, and when necessary, file those clearers down to the depth indicated by the gauge. You should also consider your own private modification to the depth of the clearers, depending on the wood you're cutting—more clearance for softwood, less for hardwood.

Tool manufacturers don't miss their chance to sell you a device for "perfect" sharpening of your chainsaw. In use, this device—a file guide—is positioned over the saw teeth; it holds the file in the proper position required for a good job. You may find such devices useful but for any sharpening of chainsaws, as with handsaws and circular saws, I prefer a freehand approach.

A FINAL WORD

Very few house and boat carpenters tackle their own sharpening jobs, but I don't fault them for it. Even when you are set up for it, saw filing can be drudgery.

The other side of the coin is that when you learn to do your own filing, you will have gained a new skill. But better yet, you might be spared hearing your favorite professional saw filer say, "I meant to file your saw last week, but Aunt Martha's big toe got infected and...."

Chainsaw—

Jointing the depth gauge—

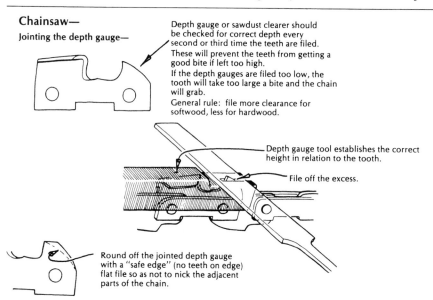

Depth gauge or sawdust clearer should be checked for correct depth every second or third time the teeth are filed. These will prevent the teeth from getting a good bite if left too high.
If the depth gauges are filed too low, the tooth will take too large a bite and the chain will grab.
General rule: file more clearance for softwood, less for hardwood.

Depth gauge tool establishes the correct height in relation to the tooth.

File off the excess.

Round off the jointed depth gauge with a "safe edge" (no teeth on edge) flat file so as not to nick the adjacent parts of the chain.

ABOUT THE AUTHOR

 Harold H. "Dynamite" Payson is a professional boatbuilder who specializes in light plywood construction, though in the past he built traditional plank-on-frame craft. Most of his boats—among them the famed Gloucester Light Dory and the Instant Boats series—are from the board of Philip C. Bolger. Many of the prototypes of Bolger's small boats have been built by Payson as part of their continuing association. Dynamite is a retired lobster fisherman, a saw sharpener, and the proprietor of H.H. Payson & Co., which offers boatbuilding plans for sale to the average boatbuilder. He is the author of *Instant Boats*, *How to Build the Gloucester Light Dory*, *Go Build Your Own Boat!*, *Build the New Instant Boats*, and a number of magazine articles. He lives and works in South Thomaston, Maine.